V. I. P.

Also by Sumana Roy

POETRY
Out of Syllabus (Speaking Tiger Books, 2019)

PROSE
How I Became a Tree (Aleph Book Company, 2017;
Yale University Press, 2021)
Missing: A Novel (Aleph Book Company, 2018)
My Mother's Lover and other stories (Bloomsbury India, 2019)

Sumana Roy

V. I. P.
Very Important Plant

Shearsman Books

First published in the United Kingdom in 2022 by
Shearsman Books Ltd
PO Box 4239
Swindon
SN3 9FN

Shearsman Books Ltd Registered Office
30–31 St. James Place, Mangotsfield, Bristol BS16 9JB
(this address not for correspondence)

www.shearsman.com

ISBN 978-1-84861-825-1

Copyright © Sumana Roy, 2022
The right of Sumana Roy to be identified as the author
of this work has been asserted by her in accordance with the
Copyrights, Designs and Patents Act of 1988.
All rights reserved.

All images in this book are by Nikhil Das
and are copyright © Nikhil Das, 2022

ACKNOWLEDGEMENTS

I'm grateful to the poetry editors of *Granta*, *Berfrois*, *Drunken Boat*, *The Modern Review*, Yale University Press blog, *Domus*, *Almost Island*, *A Letter, A Poem, A Home*, Little Toller Books, and *Kaani* for publishing some of the poems in *V.I.P.*

Contents

You Think You Can Repair Flowers / 11
Are Trees Anonymous? / 12
Tree Sap / 13
Tree Porn / 15
V. I. P. (Very Important Plant) / 17
Cactus / 18
How to Console a Dying Plant / 19
Grass / 21
I Want to Be a Tree / 23
How to Draw a Tree / 25
Moss / 27
Tree and Air / 28
God is a Vegetable / 30
How to Karaoke like a Tree / 31
Parthenium / 32
On Watering a Tree / 34
Life Science / 36
The Geometry of Trees / 37
Eating Light / 39
Fasting Without Light / 41
The Afterlife of Trees and Their Lovers / 43
Do Not Insult Death / 47
Forest / 49
Lover / 51
Root Vegetables / 53
Banana Leaf / 54
Banana Flower / 55
Salpaata / 56
Banana Trunk / 57
The Cherry Blossom on Rüttenscheider Straße / 59
Eating with Cézanne / 61
Tagore's Trellis / 63

Algae / 66
Roots / 68
Trees and Trance / 70
Weeping Willow / 72
Fern / 74
Tea Estate / 76
Laughing Trees / 78
Lemon / 79
Mint / 80
Papaya / 81
Amla / 83
Garlic / 84
Do Trees Hurt? / 85
Potato / 87
Bamboo / 89
Bamboo / 91
Asvattha / 93
Jackfruit / 94
Banana / 95
Onion / 96
Turmeric / 97

V. I. P.

Very Important Plant

'I spent several years in perfecting various instruments by which the plant attached to the recording apparatus is automatically excited by successive stimuli which are absolutely constant. In answer to this it makes its own responsive records, goes through its period of recovery, and embarks on the same cycle over again, without assistance at any point from the observer. In this way the effect of changed external condition is seen recorded in the script made by the plant itself.'
—Jagadish Chandra Bose,
Plant-Autographs and their Revelations

You Think You Can Repair Flowers

You think you can repair flowers.
You think you understand the velocity of fruition.
You put the night's fast through a sieve.
You are convinced that the desire for height is a mistake.
You argue that plants and people do not need to be tall.
You wonder whether noise ever dies.
You are angry that the road is the central metaphor of our times.
You are disgusted because it excludes trees.
You often ask about the gravity that keeps planets in place.
You think only trees know that secret, and hence their mimicry.
You hate fashion – there is nothing more artificial than horizontal stripes.
You admire the stylishness of bamboo – its minimalist extravagance.
You are confused why leaves on trees do not need clothes clips.
You come to the poet for breakfast. Trees begin eating at dawn.
You've met him before, in the impractical demand for kindness inside
    a river.
You believe that poets are priests – both rub the translucence of words.
You close your eyes when you meet him at last: he is stitching water.
You are rearranging scattered quotes in your mind. No tree is an island.
You stop to breathe, as if that would stop your ageing.
You aren't sure you've heard the poet right: "Did you oil the plants?"
You knew it once, how trees turned to oil, but in your hand is water,
    injured.
You snatch the skeleton of soap from the poet's palm.
You spit on it and the tree becomes a postage stamp.

Are Trees Anonymous?

You discover an autograph on a tree.
You know it's not the tree's –
it has no commitment to history.
Only strangers leave their names on bark.
That signature is a tease, a trace – 'I was here'.
(Which tree has ever needed to say that?)
No one else has their self-importance,
the smoke billowing silhouettes of madmen and lovers.
This they share with trees, these sky-holding people –
a flattened anonymity.

It is always a surprise, the history of anonymity.
You look at the trees, their indifference to recognition,
and you begin to see the path of evolution –
the mammal's backbone needs fame. The tree trunk none.
You've seen it behave like a time bomb,
you've seen 'Anonymous' become the name of a race.
Later, when you realise that tree leaves calibrate wind speed,
you discover that anonymity also has genres.
You sit under a tree and sneeze,
and you wonder which one is more anonymous –
the tree or the sneeze.

Tree Sap

You can tell the age of a person from how he spits.
You can see how infants are beginners –
how their drool is everywhere, how it makes mush of contexts.
And so with tree sap.
The awkward sprouting from everywhere when sapling –
stem, leaf, bud and root –
unlike an aged tree's leaks: proper, sombre, tidy,
like blowing your sap into a hankie.

With age everything turns viscous.
For hardening is a marker of age.
Knuckles, calluses, sores, scars; and the heart.
Madness is loose, fluid, it easily finds itself a home.
But not wisdom – maturity pickles, needs a container.
And so the viscosity of tree sap, the density of ageing madness.

When tree sap flows, your ignorance about the foreign grows nests.
For you are never sure whether it's a signal for beginning or end.
Sap is the tree's puppet, like tears are to the human heart.

Sap, noun and verb, and the difference in between.
Sap is loan and debt. (A half-song is also a song.
For when you are angry, you are still yourself.)

Once, the light became beautiful by resting on you.
Now it's solidified into sap, turned white.
And you've become canned food, a future without bones.

Tree Porn

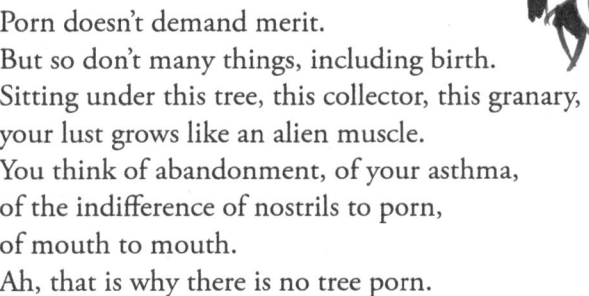

Porn doesn't demand merit.
But so don't many things, including birth.
Sitting under this tree, this collector, this granary,
your lust grows like an alien muscle.
You think of abandonment, of your asthma,
of the indifference of nostrils to porn,
of mouth to mouth.
Ah, that is why there is no tree porn.

Thoughts move like inventions, like lies:
Pornography is so provincial, it's like a tendril,
soft, looking for support, forever foreign.
For porn subverts all kinds of self-reliance –
you are dependent on the actions of others,
like a gardener's watering can or rain.

You think of migratory birds and their cycles of blind return –
how those invisible paths are unwound like bandage every winter.
In that thought is the hint of arousal, until you return to the tree.
'Tree porn is so vegan.' You prepare the line like a meal.

Bare trees aren't nudes. Porn demands such invisible note-taking.
It needs fortitude, it needs movement. It needs inflation.
Where are these in a tree? Importance is waterproof. And so is
      pornography.

It rises and settles, like clean air, losing everything, even its aged anarchy.
There's no background music, no grunt or groan.
Only wind, moving like a letter, it crumples and teases.
The tree's indifferent to hypnotism,
it doesn't care that the end is always about turning into a boat,
to reach ashore, to dress and undress, without manners.

Only humans need porn, this excess, this unnecessary.
The tree doesn't need mystery, becoming log is pornography.

V. I. P. (Very Important Plant)

You have asked this once already – why no child is ever a V.I.P.
You remember when it first came to you, this question –
when you were looking at saplings in a nursery.

Now it circulates again, like a degenerate cloud, when they report:
*"Officials in India want to make one thing clear:
the tree that President Barack Obama planted in New Delhi three weeks
ago is not dead. It just looks dead."*
A dog rushes out of you when you read it.
Is the tree a teenager, they who think of themselves as V.I.P.s?
The worry warts don't end there:
Obama planted a peepal tree at a memorial to Mahatma Gandhi.
*"By Thursday, though, it was just a single lonely stem.
Its lack of leaves has been giving Indian officials sleepless nights,
with the media in India criticising them for allowing the tree to die
less than a month after the presidential visit."*
It's as if the dying tree is a smokescreen,
or a diplomat opposing foreign policy, a new beat.

This tree, suddenly V.I.P, etiolates a new folklore.
Everyone was once born a stranger. Importance was such profligate art.
The Obama tree is dying from this accident, this post-partum depression
of being a mimic celebrity, from being a stranger to importance.

I could plant a Weeping Fig in its stead.
But even the imagination gets injured.

Fame is such a waste. It can't even be recycled.

Cactus

Because the seasons are only about the pilgrimage of water –
there's rain and there's dew,
there's the summer thirst that murmurs as beads around our lips,
and there's autumn, where water loses its feet and bones to walk as fog –
cactus must be of the water caste.

Cactus, inside which there is only one unchanging season,
like the heart which only knows the season of captivity.
Cactus, inside which water is elastic,
like a shadow that can squeeze into a gun.
Cactus, inside which all civilisation is a grandiose blur,
like dawn which humans haven't yet been able to put to efficient use.

There must be cactus.
So that we can see the seasons' sharpest edges harden into spines.
There must be cactus.
So that we can be reminded of the occasional alopecia of plants.
There must be cactus.
So that we can see a male kitchen, a permanent barbecue cooking in
      sunlight.

There must be cactus.
So that America can have her desert safety-pin lovers.

How to Console a Dying Plant

What we actually mourn is our turning to meat.
So you must never take a mirror to the dying.
For reflecting surfaces can't hold the fading of flesh.
Or even fatigue whose destiny is to never be in anyone's earshot.

The props you know are of little use.
What use are the Scriptures or the drumbeat of last wishes to a plant?
Or a hand and its show of genres – patting, holding, and then leaving?
You touch the stem from time to time, your fingers a stethoscope.
You know so little. Between your heart and head is a bed.
You fall in love often. Every day the bed turns a little more into a coffin.
Every day the plant turns a little more into an aged radio –
It will lose signal soon.

Blood, stillness, the stop of the nostril fan – these you've known as death.
But this is a foreign language: the loss of leaves, the softness of hard stem,
the collapse of the dignified vertical into the battle-lost horizontal.
And the worst – the complete rejection of water.
As if it was poison, or an unfamiliar dialect.

Death is so prolific; the death of plants a permanent epidemic.
How do you console those who do not know the fear of uncertainty?
You look for an aperture, something like an ear,
so that your words can enter the tree like an insect.
You fail, and you wonder whether insects are better consolers.
You think of things to say: the afterlife, cremation,
the crowded energies of a funeral, photographs in an album.
You stammer – what use are these to plants, to anyone?
You want to make promises about looking after its family –
swift death certificates and life insurance policies.
Instead, you look at the withering trunk
and think of how a tree has no 'spare parts', no 'organ transplants'.

Death is a tussle between law and justice.
This tree's known neither, nothing except standing.
You can't console, you can't tidy life's vanity.
For the tree, death is only an impurity.

Grass

'Egalitarian' is not a poetic word
until you benefit from its footprint.
You've imagined this of grass,
you cannot say why.

Even merit needs a shoulder.
Grass has none.
Obedience is laziness.
You've come to expect both from grass.

It annoys you, the colour blindness of grass,
its indifference to wooing the eye,
its lack of sexual energy.
You lay yourself on it but it is no woman –
there is no exchange of wetness.
Instead, winter dust asks for entry.
You sit up and suddenly there's an invasion:
Sleep fights with rock-salt thoughts, a lover's quarrel.
You touch it again, this grass, its resolute chains.
The sharpness pricks your fingers like infant teeth.
But it is passion you seek, even if violence it be.

You think of grass as human – why else their secretive lovemaking?
The sex life of parents, beggars and street dwellers
are slippery stones in your imagination. Grass is them.

Sound is indiscipline amplified to life.
You want to hear the hunger inside grass,
like your stomach's growling.
But there is no sound, none except its elasticity –
its tearing, like a bow kicking its launching string.

The heat arrives, it melts stones, roads and fat.
The earth, its host and home, scalds grass.
Blisters of yellow, ropes of stale fire, earth as ashtray.
Departure also demands craftsmanship.
And so the sameness of grass, its commune,
one worker grass blade replacing another;
like breath, undifferentiated.

Grass is always middle-aged. Like your desire.
Here, lying on it, at the eye-level of crawling ants,
you are miraculously restored as grass –
And you become the difference between 'together' and 'altogether'.

I Want to Be a Tree

I want to be a tree.

I know that this desire lives outside the curriculum.
Irrationality is man's favourite home –
One man's love is another's superstition.
I am the tree that wears passion's baggy clothes.
My hair soaks fear, my leaves the planet's poison air.
There is memory, always half-eaten,
and there's sleep, inevitably rural.
There's also sunlight, always a neighbour.
It's summer. And so the road's deathless fever.

I want to be a tree,
as naturally branched as the body's posture in sleep.
To woo birds – they avoid men and motion to sit on trees.

I'm leaning against a statue of sunlight.
The wind affects us unequally.
I wonder why tree branches
do not behave like curtains in the wind.
Or why we fail to hear creepers knocking at the door.

I want to be a tree.
The wind escaped being written.
The fire's autograph, the shrivelled sunlight on trees.
Seasons arrive like prompters in a play.
The trees perform without the need to pluck claps.
I am an extra filling out the frame.
Change, cycles, the spiky heads of moss,
the menstrual stillness and the piracy of affection.

I want to be a tree.
Air a doll between my leaves,
prayer as inconsequential as mimicry.
Only blood needs religion.
And so there is none among plants.
Only love, as accommodative as a paragraph.

Love needn't be reciprocal –
How else can we love the dead?
The earth loses ownership of dead trees.
I imagine my funeral sometimes.
You, for whom the guitar is an integer of sadness,
you who thought I was invincible like crushed paper, saying,
"My world has lost its chlorophyll".

How to Draw a Tree

The way you sometimes shout in the dark,
making of your words a torchlight with which to tear the blackness,
that is how you draw a tree.
Yes, the ear as eye; and later, spit as paint.

The tree's had its artists.
You could be a bird, who only knows the tree scalp.
You could be an earthworm, who thinks the tree is only its roots.
But you are middleman, you think the tree a person.
And so you draw it at eye level.

You know that there are many you ignore:
Nandalal, in Santiniketan, who said that a tree should be drawn like it
      grows –
from the soil to the sky;
the Europeans – draw a tree as if you were rain, pouring on it from above.
Wasn't that how the 'Nude' was born?

But you thought a kiss the best painting, lips on lips, two pairs of feet
    on levelled earth.
You wanted to create a new genre. You wanted to call it '*Equal*'.
For in no painting was the painted the painter's comrade.
You'd give it to the tree. This crumpled equality.

You loved its amateur art, you indulged its Outsider Art.
Until you saw the tree as a plagiarist.
The tree had copied itself. That is how a tree paints a tree.

All birth-giving is an experiment with *Self-Portrait*.

Moss

Moss is a good painter. It walks like art on walls.
Law only punishes effect, not process.
A garden is like law, its sling pulled for results.
And so the constant banishment of moss.

The blindness of children to its shiny green crew,
its annoyance to the eye a late adult allergy.
Walls – on them adult hands and abrasion,
scrubbing, scars and sores. The moss pogrom.
Scout. Scrape. Scratch. Abruptness is also a method.
Disappearance will always lack polish.
And so the subtraction of stains.
Histories of loss do not always foam at the mouth.
So moss waits, to return – the onanism of opportunists.

The day kills almost everything. Think of the death of dew.
The gravity of night pulls its citizens to their homes.
Darkness is moss, its roots hidden pilgrims.

You think of infant moss and wonder whether they are born as adults.
You want to know why no lover compares his woman to moss.

When moss crumbles between your fingers,
love finds a new definition: marriage is stickiness without glue.
When moss breaks from handling, you wonder why passion must
      always look for flesh.
When moss returns like a hiccup, you realise that chorus singers are
      also martyrs.
You begin to see why Anonymous is also a surname.
And you begin your demand for Moss to be a font to sign your name.

Tree and Air

Air is like a necklace.
Leaves make its beads visible.
That affectionate friction, like pearls on collar bone –
rolling, undulating, like sunsets on water.
Trees are, then, the horizon.
Air makes them so.

Wrestlers are lovers.
They test the elasticity of our bones
like lovers do the arcs of our hearts.
Air is a lover. It tests the tree's courage.

Air crumbles, no one notices.
None except trees.
For air keeps the tree alert –
like hot oil does to meat.
For the tree, air is always a foreigner.
Its bark is sentry, refusing entry to air's excess.
You notice the muscularity of air
when it teases the tree's saintly holes –
wriggling, as if it were an interview with childhood,
a question mark without a question.

The serrations on dry leaves and white clouds –
these are the ruins of air.
Like days are the ruins of time.
The dried leaves, the shape of their death,
the corpses of error, and the immortality of air.

The tree stands. Air does its homework.
It aims to give everything buoyancy.
Hair, music, laughter, the loose ends of clothes.
Even death. Ashes of burnt bodies fly away.

When you tell a story, you become air.
As reckless as rhyme, as nagging as health.
When you finish a story, you become a tree.
As self-contained as song, as patriotic as an address.

God is a Vegetable

Everything you imagine about God –
calm, stillness, nourishment, silence;
one-sided communication; lack of rabble –
you find in a vegetable.

God as man, as woman, animal, half-animal,
human without hands, penis. *God is All.*
God as noise, procession, inspiration,
rituals, priests and women's protection.
God as ruins, mid-day meal, the fast's furniture.
Door, ear, wall, fear, caricature.

God's in everything, everything breeze-torn?
Why's it difficult to look at ginger and find God in it?
Or even in peppercorn?

How to Karaoke like a Tree

There is the totalitarianism of technology.
And beneath it the sheer undergrowth of silence.
Now that silence is inside the mike, loud, stretching like a rubber band.
Once it had no pulse, not a beat except like a sip from a cup – a stop
      and home.

Think of the bad press that came its way:
Silence, sexless plateau; Silence, humourless;
Silence, sad, like eyelashes;
Silence, language uniform of church and office;
Silence, one half of a victim's proverb; Silence, Rosa Parks.

Silence – that is how you age.
Silence – that is how you become everyone.

Until the trees karaoked radioactive silence
and silence became mainstream.

Parthenium

And you thought plants had no hymen.
That the assault wouldn't show.

Animals don't spit. Not plants either.
That is the mark of the human –
as if spit and spite were related.

These thoughts prick you
as your hands brush against parthenium.
'No!' a teacher's voice calls from behind.
'Allergy!' 'Did she say energy?'

I'm not scared.
Only a masterpiece can cause allergy.

Tiny, white, like an ancient sculpture of spit.
The manners of a last bencher.
Its branches the shape of groping,
its structure a biography of curiosity.
As if even spit could have the restraint of a martyr.

Leaves like branches, the grace of breath,
the ambidextrousness of a spoon.

Parthenium.
There is no respite from education.
The nicknames soon follow:
congress grass; ganjar ghans.

I ignore their warnings.
I walk into them as if they were water –
naked in its intention, celebration its meagre purpose.

I like them, their life the colour of disaster.
They mock politeness –
they're indifferent to its price tag.
They resist plucking, the particularity of fingers.
And mouth.
Invaders. Famine weed.
They refuse to treat human skin as guest.
They don't offer the hospitality of roses.

At night, when your body becomes a landfill
and wounds return
with the mechanical energy of a funeral,
the parthenium grows on you –
first like the proscenium,
which you first misheard as its name.
A stage, noisy, waiting for silence.

The encounter is brief.
You make no memories.
Infatuation. Phantom love.
Too spacious and theatrical,
without the magnet for home-calling.

On Watering a Tree

You're slightly desperate –
you've waited too long to put 'dandruff' in a poem.

You begin watering a tree like you oil your hair.
Every pore is a bridge – wise, patient, alert.
Primitive, like the traveller's need for directions.
In this, they are life's miniature.

I look at the arms of water,
its tentacles as it emerges from the can
and scrapes the dryness of branches.

Why do we need moisture,
as if moisture were love?
Transparent, luxurious, silent.
And necessary.

You watch water wash, clean, pat
branches and leaves and the streets that connect them,
how it collects again, after the chores –
unbruised, still free, without creases.
The same water.

You carry water twice a day,
as if it were food. The tree's mealtimes.
You feel generous, like the wind which keeps ships alive.
You think of your embrace of water in every bath you take.
Your hands are touched by the memory of that gluttony.
You pour water as if you were shouting,
increasing volume (to emphasise).

What is unnecessary drains away.
And you're grateful –
for water's rationality.
Often, there are remainders –
the water-beads leap from branch to branch,
like eyes in a crowded mirror.
Only curiosity, no ambition.

You're more equal than rain –
you're a better distributor.
For often after rain you see striped trees,
stamped unequally by water.
Rain, its giant saliva.

You water a tree because you're practical.
Like a pilot who knows the value of land.

Water has its own compass.
Again, like love.
Sometimes it behaves like an owner.

This the tree doesn't know.
It thinks water is a suburb.

Life Science

Poetry is a Life Science.
You listen to its jaws.
The tongue is chloroform.
Darkness is a laboratory
where you prove your cleverness.
Every smell is a statement
you scan for taste.
Metre arranges itself like perfume.

Something is turning into a myth.

Metaphor behaves like a rug.
You check every word for extravagance,
as if they were explosives in need of detonation.
'Literature is dangerous.' That's Bataille.

Life cannot be movement alone.
Or else curtains would hurt, would bleed.
Poetry behaves like the skin of mud cake –
the movement of heat will leave cracks on it.
So you grease the moment.
You become an actor.
You choose between impulse and restraint.

Poetry is for the pure night,
both as dense as devotion.
Poems, like bottles, self-sufficient.
Yet in need of being unsealed.
Their colour unchanging –
whether empty or full.

You treat the poem like a house.
When you leave you want to turn off the lights.

The Geometry of Trees

An arc is a straight line that got bored.
It's not imperfect; it calibrates digression.

Iron is a metal that sacrificed its body.
Rust is not disease; it's a home for moist air.

The heart is not a desert.
It only shares its uncertain perimeter.

The floor is not a ceiling.
Though everything is an echo of each other.

Lines, too, must echo another.
Mirror images are, after all, only dialogues.

Trees eat light, its stubborn seeds and sex.
They've digested its fibrous rectilinearity.

The shape of branches is a weak attempt at comedy.
These, too, have angles – surprise, fantasy, uncertainty.

Every argument is a twin of another.
Grass, hair, branches – in them is air's argument.

Notice how a comb resembles hair. The disciplining
of straight lines, the comb's teeth to rhyme with hair.

Love is a shelter for the unfinished.
Branches are accidents solidified into shape.

Branches are fingerprints, unique, like a horse's gallop.
Death is the loss of shape, of intelligence, of rest.

Emptiness is a slur. No branch aims for it.
Not straight lines but blur, as anonymous as childhood.

Branches break, secrets leak, as if they were news.
This is the geometry of lines that haven't cleared their dues.

Eating Light

The harvest of appearance is our first toy.
I look at the infant and wonder –
How might a fallen fruit look at the parent tree?
Our faces are candles, light always a newborn.
The loneliness of light, of spies of beauty –
the museums inside our eyes,
the breastless trees inside them.
Where do their shadows live at night?

Trees – only trees – know that light has corners.
Our eyes are sandpaper, they blunt the edges of memory.
The world is a green room.
When I emerge out of it as a tree,
my body moves like a wrapped gift.
And I stand still, confusing bones for branches.

I imagine transparent trees.
Tree shadows are Russian dolls, hiding the plural.
I hid inside a shadow once, like animals do inside trees.
Imagine a painter hiding inside his canvas.
I was once that artist of shadows.
Darkness left me comatose.
This hunger for light, this for becoming tree.
When a sapling grows, so does its shadow.

My palm evens out everything –
cloth, soil, skin, hair.
So everything carries the weight of my hand,
everything except the tree and its accidents.
Night, I learn, is for shadows to renew their glue.
Trees do not need thermometers of privacy.
This retreat into themselves,

away from light's masturbation.
I rub my eyes, I'm wiping away what I just imagined –
sex between a shadow and a tree inhabitant.
When I close my eyes to see, again, to repeat the fishnet dream,
I only see a "No Parking" sign beside a tree's shadow.

Fasting Without Light

Every morning when you meet your shadows
you recognise them as long-lost relatives.
You notice how they too are touched by the sun's contagion.
You look at the shadows of trees climbing walls
and feel united with their rejection of goodbyes –
neither of you organises a daily funeral for sunlight.
You see the sunlight invading the field
and the grass losing its seams, its stitches.
Sunlight is more slippery than shadows,
its constancy only an illusion.
You've noticed it, like the trees,
you know about its urge to settle down, to find a home.

Darkness lives in inkpots, where does sunlight stay?
But you know that sunlight can be blind too –
it cannot see fractures in branches and bones.
You've seen it all – how sunlight makes of every plant its doll
and how darkness is a long lullaby.
All around you are the beggarly fields, scattered alms of sunlight,
the faraway moss wounded by the sun's absence in corners.
Nothing happens soundlessly –
even cream forms on milk with some sound.
And you thought tree shadows were voiceless labourers?
Something must bubble inside us – that is life.
Sap on bark, foam at the mouth; but the sweat on shadows?

The day grows old, poetry pickles in moonlight.
The tree roots end their daily pilgrimage,
the chorus of grass rebels against fonts of tidiness,
and the tree rests, at last, with its dead shadow.

The Afterlife of Trees and Their Lovers

i. Jagadish Chandra Bose's house, Mayapuri, Darjeeling

I have come here to learn a foreign language –
plants must have a mother tongue?
To the aborigines, the words for tree and house were the same.
And so this mountain house of Jagadish Chandra Bose.
It is easy to turn this into a folk tale,
to see the scientist reincarnated as a tree.
Like the seven brothers Champa?
But they were tortured; not Bose.
It is difficult to imagine a history of trees
without man in it. Man as tree, Tree as tale.

At Lloyd's Botanical Garden in Darjeeling,
I look for immigrants, plants who travelled well,
those that might have been Bose's muse –
'Plants are living things', the thought now textbook aphorism.
On my way uphill is the sacrifice of grass, the silence of soil.
Sometimes a different time zone – flowers are late risers.

I think of myths –
the forgetfulness of scientists,
jackfruit children, like Jamini Roy's 'mother and child',
gechho bhoot, ghosts of Bengali trees,
the absent-mindedness of seasonal plants.
Do these conifers remember Bose?
Or the moss on walls, the punishment for waiting?

In Bose's sparse living room, the window is a mirror.
Cleanliness has done it great violence,
the grass is now green only on the other side.
Not a pot or vase in the wooden house.
I choke on my surprise – a crematorium grows inside me.
Botany is only a history of the personality of plants.

ii. Shakti Chattopadhyay's house, Baharu, South 24 Parganas

'Are you General or Scheduled Caste?'
This is a question put to a betel nut tree in Baharu.
Shakti Chattopadhyay might have asked that question,
but would he inscribe it on the tree trunk like an insecure lover,
making the bark a government census roll?

Instead of Shakti's green room, I see red –
the soil's blood congealed into the orange flowers of Krishnachura,

the tree a leech sucking the earth's haemoglobin.
The fields in Baharu are a morgue every morning;
the sweeper deposits flower corpses in the earth's mass coffin.
Near Shakti's old house, the leaves move like flags,
like a bad mood, against the direction of thought.
Shakti knew the xenophobia caused by trees
in human spaces – beds, buses, bathrooms.
I suddenly spot trees that look suicidal,
those that Shakti might have scolded.
'Does the garden know every plant in it?'
he asked in that famous poem, you remember?

As I board the bus, I think of life insurance policies
that the drunken poet might have bought for these trees.
Later, in the parks, I only see decapitated shrubs,
green Kanishkas standing on bulldozed grass.
Every tree is a folk tale.
Only some shed their morals like leaves.

iii. Bodhi Tree, Bodh Gaya

Here you can come without brushing your teeth –
the Buddha and the fig tree have never needed toothbrushes.
The myths that surround places are like ambulance sirens –
patients, pilgrims and tourists are all the same.
One comes to trees to escape the pornography of waiting.
There must be something about sitting under a tree,
in the bandaged conflation between shade and shadow.
Other men chose exile in the forest, *vanwas* –
Rama, the five Pandava brothers, their wives.
Only Siddhartha came to a solitary tree, to escape desire.
A forest is a hiding place, where men compete with trees.
So Gautama stopped walking and closed his eyes.
The uselessness of eyes, of legs, of combs, of words –
all this the Buddha learned from this tree.

Today, only bombs are living Buddhas.
When one went off in Gaya, everyone ran,
everyone except the trees.
For death also demands walking.
Now, after the fret of flowering,
I only seek the tree's heart.
Guns are seedless fruits,
the gardens full of traitor trees.
Now I am free.
Only I know that the tree is Buddha.
And that the Buddha was a tree.

Do Not Insult Death

Do not insult death.
When a tree dies, the world becomes a chopping board.
Old scars become scabs and pain a pilgrim.
There are the houseplants, caged warriors, fighting your mission.
When leaves fall and die, history's the loneliest witness.
It grows lazier each day.
Folded clothes require less space that the unfolded.
And dead trees less than the living.

I once thought I'd have the luxury to choose my death,
at least the time of the day –
night would cause such inconvenience.
Morning preserves the dignity of death.
Death is a suitcase bursting open.
It is always readymade,
like a piece of wooden furniture.

Death and trees share similarities –
an indifference to fonts of tidiness,
to arithmetic and lies.
What separates men from trees are hiccups;
and their belief in the zero.

The children of martyrs must also be martyrs?
Where are they? Inside every boat is a tree.
Leaves, branches, and their extralegal deaths.
Jokes about hell seem aged when trees die.

I want to be a tree.
For no one's scared of a dead tree in a dark room.

Forest

Like light, you get lost in a forest.
Like light your waywardness.
You treat the forest like a book,
as if trees were chapters
that should lead to a conclusion.
You think of this forest affection
as rectilinear, but you move in circles.
You want to be light, but you become a bird,
turning the forest into a prey.

You breathe with awareness,
like you become aware of your kindness
when you drop a coin into a beggar's palm.
The old form – gasps, greedy mouth breathing.
Someone's told you that the forest is a cure.
That it's an oxygen chamber,
that it could shock your lungs into life.
Glue isn't always sticky. Think of sunlight.
The forest licks away its religion of joining.

You try to recognise the cosmopolitanism of the forest.
But you only rejoice at its rejection of the 'classic'.
You are changed without your permission
like turmeric on potatoes, they stamps on passports.
Everything sticks to lips – sap, sweat, stories.
Also this lostness, the hunting of routes a dry stain on the mouth.

To be inside a forest is to be part of an invisible autobiography.
To be inside a forest is to live in guilt –
even the unlovable must be loved.

Only light kills the annoying neutrality of trees.

There is no philosophy to explain the failure of trees,
no demand for a forest's childhood photo when it goes 'missing'.

Lover

A husband must keep secrets like a tree.
A wife must keep secrets like an earthworm.
For a happy marriage is an autumn of secrets.
Secrets are weeds that catch the traveller's eye
when you remove sacrificial naphthalene balls.
Death is a secret they must hide from each other.

Everyone gives birth – cows to cows, and grass to grass,
but only lovers can give birth to difference.
Who are the offspring of women who marry trees?
Fruits, like poetry, are always a tapeworm-sacrifice.
And so these children, not human, not plant,
but with bodies that evening news might have had,
their beings like valves, opening to only one direction.
Not hybrids but anthems, not mixture but curled maps.
They resemble thoughts left unfinished. One can never tell their age.

What separates men from trees are hiccups.
What distinguishes men from trees is their belief in the zero.
But there are also things that bind –
flowers do not grow from the same node twice;
like love cannot come from the same place again.

Once, men and women did not kiss in our movies.
Flowers pecked flowers, rose was noun and verb.
The simulated wind was passion,
rain a lover with shallow arms.
Now, suddenly, in this grown-up nation,
trees require helmets to kiss
and there are traffic jams on foreheads.
Love leaves smudges for the birth of religions.
And sex seeds, like monologues in a birdcage.

Trees do not need handkerchiefs.
Does that make them lesser lovers?

Root Vegetables

Darkness is more intimate than light.
Sadness sticks closer than joy.
Just so that taste, the righteousness, of vegetables
that grow below the earth, hidden from light.
Everything sweats in summer, everything except the darkness.
Hence potatoes, and carrots, hence their sunless irreverence.
The dew on green each morning is politically correct,
being equalist, and only a gesture.
For darkness drinks less water than light.
Darkness restricts movement –
leaves cannot move inside the earth.
The leaves and the dead – how they lie still inside it,
as if waiting for a doctor, for a knife.
You've seen it in people, those who let the sun graze on them,
and those who never emerge out of their homes;
and again those who move and walk and those who can't –
how that gives their voices and lives a postal address.
So with plants – roots are better prisoners than branches,
And going 'underground' blind metaphor.
Light nurtures beauty –
what is a potato to a cauliflower, or a lettuce to a turnip?
But darkness also has its arc. Notice the curves on a potato.
Those are the remainders of lost journeys, spent looking for light.
Hence the potato's blind eyes. The bones of darkness have punctured
      them.
When, at last, they are forced out of the ground,
they are shocked by knowledge, like a bird diving into water.
They've never known the wind – its stickiness hits them.
In the new world, they discover fire and utilitarianism,
And knowing both, realise that life is as ordinary as food.

Banana Leaf

Waxy, like the devoted slipperiness of a dancer's feet.
Striped, gently, like sunlight through a Mughal monument.
Green, as most leaves are, only less methodical
(as if it'd just been taken out of a pouch).
Delicate, like skin, like sentimentality.

I massage its creases while eating,
like music massaging my migrancy.
I trace my finger through its gutter
– the thud between its sombre reticulation –
that collects dal, gravy, and other ruins.
Before that, I watch the food on it like a witness
– the infidel yellows on pleated green;
rice, a heap, rounded, like a number;
vegetables in clusters, like groups in Parliament;
the leaking sauces, like rivers that cause wars.

My fingers skid to its margins,
to stop these wrecks from falling.
I miss the plate's opportunist rim.
It is as if it were stained glass,
only without the intimacy of that violence,
colour kicking colour, light copulating with light.

After I finish eating, it is still as innocent.
And I imagine that this is how the earth would be –
as fresh after my death, its perimeter still a secret.

Banana Flower

It arrives on my plate like a patient.
Its appearance the colour of hurt knee,
the peanuts in it like broken headlights,
the coconut scrapings unwound bandages.
I think of it before this impoverishment,
this loss in weight, shelter, and dignity.
Shelter: the maroon boat-shaped whorls,
unending barricades, like walls in ancient forts.
No, to call them walls would be too harsh.
Curtains, then? True, as nomadic as curtains,
but more protective. More affectionate,
like the cup of a mother's fingers on a tiny ear.
Inside them soldiers in saints' translucent muslin,
standing guard, shoulder to shoulder,
as if hiding something, more precious than light.
Inside every soldier is a stick, their only defence.
The cook pulls it out, castrating, then chopping.
So much is washed away: stickiness, generations,
the surprise of births.
All for food, always the gift of error.
In my mouth, a colony of iron, lying comatose.

Salpaata

Only men – and gods – need plates.
As if excess were integral to evolution.
This smoothness of plates,
as recent as hairless bodies.
Before that, before metal, before glass,
were leaves, vessels as natural as the skull and stomach.
Sal leaves, joined, like muscles, with fugitive branches,
but the stitches visible, like speed-breakers, a faint surprise.
Before the world became all consonants. An aromatic nothing.
Before our need for smoothness, for everything
to be petal, to be velvet. Like knowledge.
For living to be as seamless as light.

Khichuri understands the sentience of sal leaves
like the skin recognises a tan.
It's not the concert of rice and moong dal
as the confidence of sal leaves I taste,
mimicking light, licking it as light licked it once –
unconditionally, endlessly, almost never straying.

All things on it are dead – rice, dal, salt, sound.
But together they come alive as the dead do in art,
with grace, loneliness, and a new recognition of speed.
The food disappears as if it were a puppet.
Appetite loses its elasticity and begins to age.
When I trace the glue of starch on its skin in the end,
I see my life freckled with food, eating its only intermission.
I fold the salpaata, first folio, then quarto,
then push it in the bin as if it were a letter entering a postbox.

Then I return to news again.

Banana Trunk

At first it seems like a carapace.
And hence your indifference.
We care only for things
on which our nails can leave marks.
(The reason why our love for gold
and gravestones is fleeting.)
You're used to trunks that'll outlive you.
This softness seems illegitimate.
Layers and layers of them, soft white stems,
like milk cooling to form cream –
sediments to form rabri.
You pull – peel – each out
as if it was wrapping paper.
As if you were turning the pages of a thriller,
to smell the ending.
You break its roundness without bones,
like you make water bleed every day.

Khach khach khach khach khach khach
It could be the sound of grass
turning into logic inside a cow's mouth.
It could be a sickle mutilating weeds
under an innocent bench.
But it is this trunk, with its clots of music.
khach khach khach khach khach khach
It is perhaps duty that gives white this sound,
its own whistle, its litter of commands.
This white, luminous, like a resigned monument,
hiding life, always in decay.

At night, you bite it in your dream.
Its crunch between your teeth returns –
first cheap, then energetic,
sticking to your tongue like broken glass,
remaining what it always was:
rumour-white, the sound of an accident.

The Cherry Blossom on Rüttenscheider Straße

The poems – Thomas and Housman and Neruda –
lapsed into tourism when I first saw you,
as tall and foreign as the name,
on Rüttenscheider Straße.

Imagine impossibilities,
convicts of the imagination –
the statue of a sneeze,
a hiccup, a fall, a word escaped,
the mind unable to hold it back,
like the earth pulls back the grass.
Fleeting, floating, like a yawn.
Your life, only as long as a clap,
in a world where everything's long,
as long as struggle.

The mumble of shy pink,
the loyalty of softness,
of petals pretending to be strong,
as strong as a vow.
The hamlet of pale flags,
the glance of toothy flowers.
A collective of spring winks.

I remember the voltage –
the lifespan of a blink.

But that is not what I saw.

When I saw you, I saw Time.
Time, our primitive invention.
I'd been counting wrong all my life.
You stood there,
Time bruising your flowers.
You stood there,
keeping time in colour, like aging hair.
I still remember you ten years later,
standing, flickering like impulse,
breathing brevity, skeletons of coral air.

Eating with Cézanne

i. Peach

'See how the light tenderly loves the
apricots, it takes them over completely,
enters into their pulp, lights them from
all sides! But light is miserly with the
peaches and lights only one side of them.'
      Cézanne

War-veteran fine fuzz.
My fingers compare dampness.
Humans sweat. This is the timid vapour of fruit,
measured, like the weight of water in a sigh.
A selfish curve. The pride – its accent – of being fruit.
That dimple, a scar – from gobbling light.
The skin, holding back taste till the end.

ii. Apple

'You wretch! You've spoiled the pose. Do I have to tell you
again you must sit like an apple? Does an apple move?'
      Cézanne

The shape of ceremony.
As simple, as self-assured.
As tight as a bite.
Red, not theatre but of a hard pinch.
Freckles, unapologetic, like death.
Skin, drunken but crisp.
Its texture like water waxed by swimmers' arms.
Still; meditative and unmoving like a nose.

iii. Carrot

'The day is coming when a single original carrot will give birth to a revolution.'
                    Cézanne

Its hidden life, as boneless as darkness.
Sunlight solidified into candle, inverted,
the tip a wick sniffing for light in the soil.
Much later, you remember something missing –
the intimacy of seeds.
Its flamboyance, as if only for the backstage.
That colour, the instinct for storage, of unused light,
of rage, its crunch, stunned into unashamed strength.

iv. Cucumber

'But a touch of green, believe me, is enough to give us a landscape,
just as a flesh tone will translate a face for us.'
                    Cézanne

Green, urgent green. The green
wrapping white translucence within.
A scab. A wound. White blood.
Viscous, like traffic.
A thin slice, one more, then many.
Like green kohl-lined eyes.
Time moves like smoke,
the eyes water, the slices go limp.

Tagore's Trellis

i. *Saptaparni*

Like cooking oil brings everything together,
green emulsifies everything.
Even odd numbers. Three. Five. And seven.
You renamed plants like a doctor changing a drug.
Names, their feet-dragging newness, would be cure.
This had many already: blackboard tree, devil tree;
in Bangla, a bedroom's comfort in the word: *chhatim*.
Alston saw the bark for making blackboards,
producing scholars, and so *Alstonia scholaris*.
In Hindi, *shaitan*, devil.
The paralysing dusk in the smell of its flowers.
Your father sat under them – *chhatim-tala* –
and the smell of inexperience overwhelmed him.
He mistook it for the fragrance of rest,
for the initials of stillness.
You, artist of the skeletons inside light,
saw the leaves – the outstretched palm.
Beggar's palm, so needy that five fingers weren't enough.
Sapta – seven. The midrib, arched,
like a poor man's hunger.
The leaves like windowpanes,
with exactly their confidence –
they know light will enter them.
You stained them with achievement,
you turned them into laurel,
you made them a stopwatch of learning.
A saptaparni leaf in every graduating student's hand.
Not the weather of education,
not pond, not plough, not metal, not machine,
but language, as colloquial as the wind,

and vision, as green as incompletion.
That is why you chose the saptaparni –
to give a number, a pin code, to habit,
to remain vulnerable to discolouration.

ii. Malatilata

Oi malatilata dolay
Piyalotorur kolay...
– Rabindranath Tagore

Not its determined fragrance that curves into the nose,
reminding you of something unused,
not its pink and white petals, always on the verge of injury,
not its long stalk, without a knee.
You only saw the breeze, its voice filled with water?

Now, that is all I see too –
not the hesitant flowers,
but how they whip the air,
how their dance creases the wind.
The breeze, like a cufflink,
bringing them together – the smell and my nose.
The breeze, like a missionary, weighing the flowers.

As evening descends, to strike root,
a task it attempts without success every day,
their scent grows stronger, more obsequious.
But it is your Pilu that gives them oars –
they swim in the air, they rest, they float.
Then Kaharwa gives them feet, they hurry,
and soon, after being orphaned by speed,
they fall, like silence, ignorant of falling.

Algae

Here they are –
as smooth as death, as calm as the ignorant;
the music of algae in a lap of blue,
in the province of Anna Atkins's photogram.

In all of these – a blue film;
cyanotypes, as if that name was necessary
to stress its seriousness –
is the insurance of memory.

Algae.
So many firsts –
the first photogram;
the first division of the plant kingdom.
The myths of the first boy in class,
of origin, and algae's absentmindedness.

And the confusion
(like identifying a perfume from a fragrance) –
plant or animal?
Algae, either and or, always swimmer,
always the wind in wind-ow;
algae, crossing borders without ceremony.
Now they treat you as lab animal,
as synecdoche for water,
as if your nose was pressed against glass,
as if you were your own public.

I don't need to know this.
I don't care for the hygiene of information.
(Only once, when reading Fanon, I wondered –
Does Algiers get its name from algae?)

Now all knowledge is a suburb to the self.
There's only the elasticity of this picture –
the inheritance of its foreignness,
the panic of chlorophyll when meeting light,
the vulnerability of attachment,
its dunking in gravity like a lost bird;
losing dimensions, flattened like a blink
until suddenly awake, like a tickle –
the transformation of Laminaria digitata
into Matisse's *Blue Nude*;
the psychology of the first life on earth
captured as in an inkblot test.

Roots

For an ant this is a cathedral.
It's being treated as a pariah.
It waits for a sound –
religion is about overhearing.

The ant wants entry.

Roots are comic, like religion.
Everything invisible is comic –
light, love, vapour, god, ghost.
And roots, hidden, like breath.

The confidence of soil,
the openness of water,
the stubbornness of pebbles.
These the ant knows.
But all old knowledge is useless –
it only lights the street, not the house.

The ant wants entry.

The sweetness of light, its seeds
and scales, gives the soil chronology.
For anything outside light has nothing,
no skin, no appetite, and no history.

The ant wants entry.

How well the roots fit into the soil –
space as well-utilised as in a hotel room.
Its tightness, without excess, like a sentence.
There's no centre, as if it were oil.

The ant wants entry.

Death violates us, exposes orifices.
Roots shrivel, the soil releases its prisoner.
Ants rush to occupy the slum.
Converts, they treat roots as outcasts.

Back to your roots:
A new religion is born.

Trees and Trance

Material, not ambition, produces difference.

There's the fading thhoop-thhoop of the washerman,
And the dust-demolishing blitz of the washing machine.

The insistent beating-resting-knocking of the hammer,
And the shrill humourless piercing of the drilling machine.

The tail-dragging shyness of the broom, its tiptoeing grace,
And the apocalyptic barking of the vacuum cleaner.

The lullaby-rhythm of the shil-nora, the slow blink of a dheki,
And the crushing-razing flagellant inside the grinder.

The intimacy of pen scratching paper, sealing silence as on an envelope,
And the clerical tapping on the keyboard, turning writers to woodpeckers.

The bass of the comb after the towel's silent soaking of wet hair,
And the cyclonic turbulence of the hair dryer, its vanity in hot force.

The refined breathing of the hand-fan, mimicking the negative,
And the nagging whirr of the electrical fan, stinging the air.

The wordless calling for attention, in love or in hurt,
And the bodiless bleating of the calling bell.

Inwardness, not material alone, produces difference.

There's the shrubby head-banging that punctuates trance music,
And the scalar head-swaying of trees where all wind is always aalap.

Weeping Willow

"For now, I think, it is best not to hold literature in overly high regard. Studying literature doesn't benefit the war. At best, a war song, if written well, can be read while resting between battles and may provide some amusement. To put it somewhat more grandly, it's like planting a willow tree: once it has grown tall, providing broad and dense shade from the sun, the farmers, having ploughed until noon, might sit under the tree to eat their meal and rest."
—Lu Xun, 'What is Revolutionary Literature?'

Even tears have genres.
You know them from the way they flow.
(Or refuse to.)
Sticking to eyelashes like a water pimple,
meandering like a new river,
creating ox-bow lakes on your cheeks,
the salt hardening like egg white on skin.

This is the thing about tears –
how they come from different sources
but end up in the same bin: the eyes.
Just as so many agricultural fields end up in our gullet.

You turn to trees to look for the same –
the dust of elsewhere in the freckled wind,
the anger of temporary famines in their roots,
the complaint of stars in the light travelling from the sun.

You wonder whether tears are alliteration, the erupting sameness.
Was it this that gave it its name – Weeping Willow?

Kisses, sorrys, consolation, promises.
How do you offer these to a weeping tree?
You pat, you tap, those palindromes;
you blow foo foo – for something to evaporate.

You've noticed how no one cries in official photographs.
Tears devalue you, like torn clothes.
Tears must be like roots – hidden.

This winter tree's baldness, its lack of nook to hold affection
(For affection needs edges, to collide,
and crevices, to collect, like the heart and mouth).
This is how the leaves grunt and fall.
This is how the butchery of hurt is performed.
This is how tears displace air.
And this is how Salix babylonica, always female, weeps –
losing parts of its body, like the mind once lost itself in the postbox.

Fern

i. Fiddlehead Fern

The tiny leaves in shirshasana,
coiled like a Swiss roll,
hesitant to be leaves.
The stem as tender as a waist.
Bend, break, chop, fry –
juicy, muscular, as full as an epitaph.

The curls like solidified sea waves,
only green, hence more naked.
This is a plant in a time before underwear.
It rejects sculpture –
when you pull its placenta-leaves,
it returns to its foetal position.
That is its privilege, the privilege that is poetry.

ii. Tree Fern

Here is a joint family.
Beside it are its photogenic shadows.
It could also be a building –
a long verandah opening into a series of rooms.
But it is a fern.
Here is its stem, as responsible as sleep,
holding leaves which mimic each other.
The serrations on its leaves, first like reptile teeth,
then a window that is scared to open,
as if the air was police.
One leaf on each side,
Socratic, like a dialogue.
Only one, at the top, without a companion.
Like a leap year,
unsure of what to do with an extra, that surplus.

Tea Estate

It sometimes seems as absurd as sleep –
this forfeiting of control over one's body.
This sacrifice of leaves every day,
as swiftly replaceable as bed linen.
And even more surprising,
its immediate filling-in,
like a waiter filling a half-empty glass.

The chorus in the tea estate before noon –
the sound of plucking, like cushions losing air,
leaves cryptic with moisture.
That susurration, as if water was an ornament,
like an anklet measuring distance with sound.

The razed heads of tea bushes –
the failure of comparisons: lawn? carpet?
Beak-like leaves sprouting, visible,
like a solitary chair in a bare room.
And the related curiosity –
why the mind likes to rest on flat surfaces.

The smell of tea leaves is an accent in your breath.
It wakes you up, bruises your memory,
like a hot wok wakes up oil.
You put your palm on the tea bush –
there is no theatre. It's not a fireplace.
Saliva flâneurs inside your mouth.
You're drinking with your nose,
and now with your fingers.
The pulse of leaves stains your mouth.
This bony aroma becomes your guide.

The inside of your mouth is a scar –
tea's bitten it fondly, like a pet dog.

You leave like light, without warning.
The jeep vomits scales of smoke.
And you're still surprised
by how articulate the tea leaves were.

Laughing Trees

Laughter needs a face.
And the chords of vowels.
(Ha ha he he hi hi ho ho hu hu)
Laughter comes from memory,
from fear, from imagination,
from the hostility of comparison.
These trees are yet to know.

Light, air, water, attention – life's hologram.
Laughter, as useless as kisses,
as two-dimensional as talent.
A social invention, an unequal affair.
Laughter's an animal without feet
in a room that only has chairs.

Leaves shrivel faster than flesh.
They take second-hand shapes –
the arc of smiles, as brittle as absence.
As if only death were the right furnishing
for laughter.

Laughter has no unit. Like anonymity.
Who knows whether trees laugh –
laughter's an accident in this vaccinated city.

Lemon

The first taste always feels like mishearing.
So you pause to check,
you lead your tongue there again,
as if you were re-reading.
Every consequent bite is an echo,
a delay of something promised but unfulfilled.
You know the taste is ad hoc.
So you give it tenancy –
it teases, it cleans, it behaves like an actor.
And just when it's about to disappear,
it seems like the coming of light,
of a window growing,
caramelising into a door.

You lick again.
The rind has the dignity of a doll.
The tongue brushes past it –
bitter wrapping paper.
Lemon is old-fashioned –
its hair is parted in the middle.
The sour hum grows predatory –
a drop becomes a bath inside the mouth.
Errant, it wakes up remote places.
Its smell is a hyperbole,
it leaks into your afterlife.
It squirts into the eyes
– what is good for the mouth
isn't necessarily good for the eye –
and light suffers a miscarriage.

Mint

It now seems natural, in retrospect,
that leaves should taste of water.
But only here is it condensed,
heightened, as anxiety is in newspapers.
That everyone, including water,
should be eligible for transformation
is natural. But that water, colourless
and aroma-less, could turn green
is mint's phantom artistry.
This fragrance, like a halo,
the veins of water distilled
into this young smell,
boyish and sacred,
the moment before it turned sacred,
the aroma of impermanence.
It is the fur of water,
converting its religion,
that tickles your nose.
Bruised, it fights the enemy with its smell,
further seducing its assassin.
Like pus, this smell stains the air.
The air, so long its plaster cast,
is ripped open by a knife.
The fibres of fragrance burst,
like a sky scratched by wind –
wild in pain, the delight of death.
Water, migrant species, moves
from the leaves to your tongue.
Inside your mouth,
the leaves lose their sails.
The ship of death crashes against teeth.
'There is no port, there is nowhere to go…'

Papaya

Pakhi paaka pepey khaaye
Pakhi paaka pepey khaaye
Pakhi paaka pepey khaaye

That metallic tongue twister,
before its first taste on my tongue.
So a bird, and henceforth, only animals:

a Trojan horse, when Ma split it open,
the seeds Trojan soldiers, unmoving,
glued by pins and needles;

a little later, many frog eyes,
the suspicion confirmed,
when they jumped out of our hands,
like frogs must, slimy from rest;

the peel like an insect in camouflage,
pleating light, soaking and leaking,
green, yellow, as if colour were a prison,
light resting, exhausted of travel;

the skin a dragonfly without humour.

The flesh as if saffron moss,
its taste coming from stillness,
only smoother, without body hair,
as cool as an air-conditioned slipper.
The sweetness a matter of speculation –
black ants must taste as sweet?
Moderate, gentle, like bird feather.
Its taste as balanced as an afternoon.

Now I only remember the seeds,
as unnecessary as snoring is to sleep,
and crowded, like knowledge.

Amla

That light might have a bitter taste
comes to you when you bite a gooseberry.
The crunch, like a creaking gate, forced to yield;
the membrane, like a thread of fat on a cooled gravy,
as if light were an animal cooked like meat.
The tartness, relentless, the tongue in meditation,
like a wet log catching moss.
Sour, swimming in sensuous circles.
The taste unbuttoning, arriving slightly late,
as if it was its destiny to be anachronistic.
The first pungency turned to petition, for change,
the surrender to the acetic,
the juice creased with surprise.

And when you think eating's over,
realising that it isn't very different from fasting,
sweetness comes unbidden, first like an annexe,
then taking over, until you're even jealous of your spit –
it is sweeter than all the playfields in your body.

Garlic

In this photograph the garlic is a skull cap,
the translucent skin like fragile lace;
the cloves suburbs coming together,
as on a journey out of town;
the spine an umbrella stick,
or, as if the whole bulb was a carousel.

But garlic is not for fancy dress.

It's the dominating partner in a relationship –
overpowering, hasty, feverish.
Its diaspora extends beyond the plate,
to fingers and the cowardly air.
Scared of none
– hot oil, knife, the dead, or digestion –
it loses its body with confidence,
not like a martyr but like a child,
hypnotised by the need for transformation.

Do Trees Hurt?

Hurt manifests itself in primary colours –
red, blue, yellow.
Blood; numbness; bile.
There's white and there's black,
the two extremes,
like hats and shoes – life and death.

And waiting before you is life,
as inexhaustible as colour.

You've never seen a heart –
this port of limbs and wrecks,
its scars, its nails that rust inside you,
inaudibly, but scrape its skin
even when you pad it with the grease of forgetting.

That is why you want to be a tree –
to be free of injuries, of servility,
of beds that hold the foetus of your fears.
Its cambium records years, time as vermicelli,
but not hurt's ageism, not grief that clogs truth and rivers.
Its roots, that comb and grope, as if water was a secret love,
its leaves that get dressed for air,
flowers who know that sorrow is a wilderness,
fruits whose dimpled skin is a leftover of absence,
and seeds, who, like pain, are Lazarus –
they return every year, hoping that knowledge
would make them better warriors.
Their memory fails them – they've forgotten nakedness,
like adults who think it's luggage.

I don't know whether trees hurt.
I only remember Dida's words to me at nine:
'Only those who bathe can cry'.
Dadu, never far away, correcting her,
'Only those who're anonymous don't hurt'.

Potato

It is 1984.
The ink of soil is dressing our nails,
its sweat sniffing our feet.
The weight of discovery's a blanket on our shoulders.
My grandfather is torturing the soil.
He wants the potatoes to behave like athletes.

I'll soon be ten, my brother eight.
We're still friends. We still share a bed.
We lie like gravestones beside each other at night.
We fight like the wind during the day.
We're angry that we'll be siblings all our life,
that there is no retirement age to this relationship.

But here, near grandfather's pond in Hili,
we are fish looking for our lost scales.
We've never seen a village.
We think it a flaw, we complain.
We think it a holiday, we treat it like a wallet.
Everything is new for us, even this sharp water,
which behaves like bandage.

Grandfather wants to be a grandfather –
he scolds his son to claim ownership,
and soon our father is no longer ours.
We watch our father's anger slip into a coma.
He likens our bodies to empty bottles,
our thinness becomes a disease, the city's fault.
Our bodies need soil, soil and potatoes,
potatoes, where soil's talent is condensed.

And so we go to the pond –
its arteries green with slime.
Grandfather holds me like a fritter
and dunks me into the pond.
My flat chest crashes against the flat chest of water.
Only one of us is breathless.
My limbs become horns, honking for freedom.
My brother runs away.

We meet at last, our hips on the soil.
Suddenly, the soil seems funny.
We scrape and dig and fight its tightness.
My brother and I laugh – we'll win this tug of war.
We pull the head of leaves with all our might.
But all effort's a waste – we could be pulling sunlight.
We bend and squat and probe and scratch,
we say Shh-Shh, trying to catch it unaware.

Until the soil explodes and the potatoes emerge
like grooms. The elasticity of our joy bursts.
We fall to the ground, fattened by laughter.

Bamboo

We like things without bones.
We like things that dissolve inside our mouths
the way life seems to have dissolved into this world.
For death might not have touched every region,
a napkin, a part of a mirror, newly-born memory,
but life's business is everywhere.
Life's business is in bones.

We like things without bones.
We want affection to be boneless,
only muscles, like an elephant's trunk.
We distrust bones – life passes through them,
hidden, like cunning. They break without reason, like retirees.
But also return, as if after an interval.

We like things without bones.
Except when they are bamboo.
Then we dislike the encumbrances of flesh,
when meat and bone become one and the same,
like comedy, grief inseparable from laughter.
Anything without grease will curl –
dry hair; that must be how the heart acquired folds.
Love is grease, it hydrates.
Its bones are invisible, as in water.
Bamboo, oily to the touch, straight, without curls –
love has given it form, without dust, without curtains.

Love is a womb, a paunch. It has no bones.
And so the hollows of air that break speed, like love,
waiting between nodes, bamboo's cheekbones.
Bones give sophistication, form; marriage wants to be bony.
But bamboo only waits for a season without bones,

a season as spineless as the sky or dreams,
and finding none, it rests at last –
erect, wondering whether shoes have bones.

Bamboo

Bare-limbed, motionless, prop and protagonist,
it stands, as if mimicking its own sculpture,
holding its breath permanently,
immune to fatigue.

(Occasionally, only occasionally, fugitive leaves –
leaves like bird beaks, open, always hungry.)

(Its node-knots, soft, but only to the eye –
like a girl's first sense of her breasts.)

To be able to reduce a life to two lines
requires the grace of darkness.
||
Only parallel lines are resistant to shock –
anything that is joined will break.

Time bleaches away colour –
hair loses its blackness,
the sky its ceremony,
the greenness of bamboo is taken away.

And when you begin to see it as human,
you look for a flaw, the biography of an accident.
Not finding any, you try to move it,
like parting a woman's legs,
and the question arrives without air –
How would one make love to a bamboo?

Asvattha

You've taken your name literally:
Asvattha: under which horses stand.
And so the tireless gallop in your leaves;
their tips – like horsetails – are wind vanes.
They flicker as if it was a rehearsal for a storm –
but it's true, every moment is a rehearsal of death.
No, they're perhaps rehearsing life:
movement is a prison they want to be freed from.
The leaves are moving – like tongues, like time, like tradition,
like things rise inside an oven, soft and curious.
The leaves are moving – they're like smoke,
always waiting for the wind to push them.
The leaves are moving, the light is dying,
they are surrendering to rambling darkness,
to its intimacy which preserves constancy.

The leaves are moving though I can't see them.
They'll be there tomorrow, I know –
like me, they have nowhere to go.

Jackfruit

This is not a fruit.
It is the Buddha's head:
dots, mounds, spikes – his curls,
as in the Gandhara statues.
When the skull cracks open,
smell stretches its legs,
flies panic, overdose on bushy sweetness.
That voluptuous yellow, sweetened light,
large-cheeked sweetness;
as if sweetness was a muscle.
Why is our blood salty but theirs sweet?
Juice, as viscous as fever,
never unreluctant to pause, to stick.
The seeds emerge out of the fibrous pulp
like Bodhisattvas, slippery but sincere –
not yet monk, not yet saint,
just anaesthetised by wonder,
unsure whether life was a second-hand thing.

Banana

I think that it's a miracle
our legs don't collide when we walk.
My nephew walks two bananas as if they were legs,
then turns one loutish – it kicks the other.
It lands on the table – not blood but mucus splatters.
The little boy invents a parent, and soon, a doctor:
a spoon lifts it up, a caring father. Napkins are bandage.
There is silence – the routine sound of an emergency.
The empty peel lies like a bird with broken wings.
My nephew touches it with his tongue –
the taste of a bruise. He pushes it away –
no, pain isn't to his taste.
The other banana is now in his hand:
hunchback, as if born old.
'Statue,' he certifies, for no reason.
The emptied peel's like an unwashed milk bottle –
only more bereft, more broken.
My nephew holds the two bananas side by side.
I wonder whether one of my legs is shorter than the other.
He rolls his fingers over one with all his strength,
as if it were a lid he was trying to open.
He eats – his mouth's like a loom.
In his bite's the sound of squishy mud.
The bananas are walking again.

Onion

Amar e dhup na poraley, gondho kichu naahi dhaley,
Amar e dweep na jalaley, dei na kichui aalo
Ei korecho bhalo, nithuro hey
Nithuro hey, ei korecho bhalo…

(How'd there be fragrance if I didn't burn like incense
How'd there be light if I didn't burn like a lamp
You've done the right thing, O Cruel One…)
 —Tagore song

I watch them lose water and shrivel,
lose colour, lose a couplet's sting,
lose secrets, lose dusk.
I remind myself that they're dying –
curved, nail-like julienned onions,
tiny twigs crawling on a frying pan.
Oil tickles the back of the onion slivers,
they crumple into ancestral shapes of escape –
broken wings; a half-grasp; collapsed joints.
Once pink procession, now broken barbed wire.
Death is such a spendthrift.

Of everything, this most precious –
the release from the burden of form,
of slivers becoming thread; life is too hard.
An onion's arcs, its whorls, its caves –
the weight of form:
water's invisible scaffolding.
Then, this boneless rest –
death changes everything,
including handwriting.
Inside my mouth caramelised onions,
the obscene sweetness of death –
as if death were a fruit that's ripened from waiting.

Turmeric

That desire is not separate from deprivation
becomes visible in your body –
how darkness, its craving
for the sky's adolescent light,
coagulates into your form.
And hence your roop –
a different shape in every incarnation,
its bends and gouts and calluses
a hardened memory of your journey inside soil,
of the greed for light, its lace,
through accidents, against pale reason.

Turmeric.
Terra merita. Meritorious earth.
I think of the origins of your English name
as I peel your skin. The terra falls off.
The merit stains my fingers.

Haldi.
The fifty-three names in Sanskrit –
in them a cosmology of human arms:
of rubbing and grinding,
of digging and dyeing…
They, these names, like planets,
related to each other,
only through distance –
gauri, bahula, bhadra,
haridra, dear to Hari, your Krishna;
the intestines of yellow
explode from the nest of these names.
Yamini and Nishakya, Ratrimanika –
the damp grace of darkness rests in them,

the memory of soil, its flint blindness.
There are others that lie like slate –
starched with expectation:
to stain is the mark of being alive;
every colour is an inflammation,
of something peeling away,
the hardware of life.

At night,
inside the sternness of the dark,
I think of these names and the European –
the White saw merit in you: *Terra merita*;
here, with skin as brown as yours,
and our insides thatched with yellow,
we called you everything,
synonyms and opposites,
Kaveri and Vairagi,
prostitute, and one free of desire…

One saw merit, the other maya.

www.ingramcontent.com/pod-product-compliance
Ingram Content Group UK Ltd.
Pitfield, Milton Keynes, MK11 3LW, UK
UKHW040238250426
12048UKWH00043B/1577